Liturgical Space & Church Re-ordering

Issues of good practice

CHURCH OF IRELAND PUBLISHING

Published by
Church of Ireland Publishing
Church of Ireland House
Church Avenue
Rathmines, Dublin 6

Designed by Susan Hood
Cover design by Bill Bolger

© Representative Church Body, 2010

All rights reserved. No part of this publication may be reproduced, stored in or introduced into a retrieval system, or transmitted in any form or by any means (electronic, mechanical, photocopying, recording or otherwise), without the prior written permission of both the copyright owner and the publisher

ISBN 1-904884-34-7

Printed by Paceprint Trading Ltd,
Dublin, Ireland

Table of Contents

Preface 5

1. Setting the Scene 9

2. Contextual Questions 15

3. Practical Application 21

4. Wider Considerations 27

Bibliography & Resources 33

Appendices:

I Six practical steps for re-ordering of churches in the Republic of Ireland 38

II Seven practical steps for re-ordering of churches in Northern Ireland 40

Preface

IN 2009 THE LITURGICAL ADVISORY COMMITTEE, conscious of the lack of any official guidelines in the Church of Ireland concerning matters of church re-ordering and liturgical space, laid some preliminary reflections before the General Synod. This document was commended for study throughout the Church and responses were invited — the contents of which could be taken into account before a final text was produced. A sense was developing that the considerable emphasis placed upon liturgical texts in the years prior to 2004 needed to be followed up by some theological refection upon the context and space in which these texts are normally used. We were also conscious that there have been a number of re-ordering and building schemes in various parts of the Church in recent years, in which those involved recognised that they had to plan in something of a vacuum for lack of clear advice based on liturgical principles.

What follows is a careful reworking of the 2009 proposals, approved by resolution of the

General Synod in 2010. This is not statutory material, but it is published with the authority of the General Synod as representative of the Church's current thinking on this matter. Hence the guidelines have some measure of authority. They will, we hope, provide useful advice for select vestries, diocesan councils and architects when church building development or re-ordering is being contemplated. Their contents can be fruitfully shared with planning and heritage officials in order to establish fertile common ground in the context of which appropriate works may be authorised. Vital to the process of producing these guidelines has been consultation not just among liturgists and within the church, but also with the statutory authorities with whom we are required to co-operate in schemes of this kind. We therefore owe a particular debt of gratitude to the Heritage Council of Ireland and within it to Mr Colm Murray.

Because the Church of Ireland has such an abundance of old buildings, it is inevitable that the adaptation of liturgical space to meet today's requirements for worship will, in most cases, have to be done in centuries-old churches

– the atmosphere and style of which demand respect. However we are anxious to show how such buildings can meet the unfolding needs of our time, if the work carried out is of suitable quality and sensitivity, and we feel it is important that parishes are encouraged not simply to baulk at the concept. We also feel strongly that, as in past generations, the churches in which we worship need to receive the artistic imprint of our generation not least so that future worshippers will be able to reflect on the art that inspired and challenged us.

We wish to thank those who made submissions to enrich our work, and we offer these guidelines as a small contribution to what the *Book of Common Prayer, 2004,* describes in its Preface as 'a fresh experience of the beauty of holiness'.

Having been approved and ordered to be published by authority of the General Synod 2010, the text has now been brought into printed format, and we are grateful to Church of Ireland Publishing, and Dr Susan Hood, Publications Officer, for bringing this to fruition.

Liturgical Advisory Committee, August 2010

1
Setting the Scene

THE *BOOK OF COMMON PRAYER*, **2004**, (hereafter *BCP*, 2004) — the texts of which were all ratified by the Church of Ireland General Synod — combines the traditional forms of worship from our past with contemporary modern language rites. Common Prayer was the vision of the compilers, who sought to 'unify the worship of God's people, while allowing reasonable scope for diversity within the essential unity of the Church's prayer.'[1]

It was their hope that the texts of our worship 'should properly articulate and embody the Church's faith', and 'have the capacity to draw God's people in our time to a fresh experience of the beauty of holiness.'[2] At the request of the General Synod, the Liturgical Advisory Committee has prepared this document following reflection, both consequentially and theologically, about the potential of liturgical space.

---

[1] *The Book of Common Prayer 2004* (Dublin, 2004), the Preface prefixed at the revision of 2004, p. 7.
[2] *ibid.*

Liturgy is a word which means the *work of the people* in the particular sense of their public service to God. It has been the committee's aim to see how the available space in our church buildings, together with their furniture and fittings, might best facilitate the expression of our Church's faith, as well as enhance the worship experience of the people of God. The texts within the *BCP*, 2004, should harness the visual, liturgical and architectural assets of each particular church as part of the whole act of worship, prayer and proclamation, with the emphasis on the balance of Word and Sacrament.

Throughout the Church of Ireland there is great diversity of worship. In addition to the choice of traditional or modern language orders of service, we recognise that styles of worship may be influenced by a whole range of factors including the following:

- the age and style of the building,
- the size and age range of the congregation,
- whether there are musicians available,
- the tradition of churchmanship,

and many others…

Yet despite this diversity, the commonality of the prayer enshrined in the *BCP*, 2004, is an instrument of unity.

The following guidelines therefore aspire to focus on the unity in diversity which enriches our communion as a Church, while setting out some general guiding principles for parishes to consider for themselves. These are based on the various elements of our orders of service within the *BCP*, 2004, and challenge us to look afresh at how our worship and faith within a particular location may most effectively engage with the worship space to the glory of God.

Over the centuries church buildings have been erected with definite theological assumptions that motivated their designers, however much such people were actually aware of this. Fundamental to understanding why churches are ordered in a particular way is knowledge of the local environment and past theological perspectives. Architectural styles, fixtures and fittings and internal layout often reflect more than a general Church of Ireland way of doing things. They may represent a local churchmanship, may be important examples of local styles, may use significant local materials and may also be the product of local patronage or design. Moreover, and more sensitively, particular items may be gifts from church members or memorials to former parishioners.

Information on such matters may be gleaned from architectural drawings, vestry minutes, episcopal visitations and other descriptive survey material, photographs and local church histories. The Church of Ireland is fortunate that vast resources of this nature are available and centrally collected in the Representative Church Body Library. Further information about the library and accessing its collections is provided in the Bibliography & Resources section at the end of this booklet.

Bearing the contents of these resources in mind, it becomes clear that modern re-ordering can jar if it is done without awareness of the original theological premise associated with the construction of the church building, and it can also be done in a purely pragmatic or functional way, without much sense of spiritual continuity or real consideration of the theological statement we would wish to have the building make today. In addressing the issue of re-ordering, questions are raised about what we wish to say to the world about the vocation of the church in our time. This needs to be done in a manner that is not the slave of contemporary aesthetic/liturgical fashion on the one hand or is timidly conservative on the other. Choices made in our time in relation to our buildings, especially when considerable capital expenditure is involved, must not be confined to cautious maintenance, but should also involve enrichments that are judged – in so far as is humanly possible – to have enduring value and staying power.

2
Contextual Questions

It is important to emphasise that church buildings are, first and foremost, places of worship. Liturgy and its practice demand a context and that context is affected by and in turn affects the delivery and experience of the act of worship. We must always remember that the Church is essentially the people rather than the building. Therefore the needs of the people and their worship must have priority. There is a need for a balance to be struck between respect for the heritage and tradition of the church building and the current requirements of its worshipping congregation. Often a congregation is torn between seeking to continue to worship in a building which they have inherited and using a liturgy which seems to demand a change of shape and furnishing in the building.

'Common' prayer means the full participation of the whole people of God, and the shape of the liturgical space should allow the full participation of the whole assembly. Many worship spaces were created in a context where there was a clear demarcation between those who led the worship and those who 'attended'. Today's liturgy presupposes a celebration by the whole people of God, the worship leaders' role being to facilitate that celebration.

How does the liturgical space in your church building measure up to that demand?

Gathering
- Does the building allow members of the congregation to gather and identify with one another as the people of God?
- How do the number and shape of the seats facilitate or restrict the gathering?
- Is there any flexibility in the seating arrangements?
- From where is the gathering part of the liturgy conducted?

Proclamation & receiving of the Word
- What genuine justification is there for having more than one focus of the Word?
- Is there a necessity to retain lectern, pulpit and reading desk?
- Where are the Scriptures read from and why?

- Is there a balance in the visual presentation of Word and sacrament? And if not, how could that be achieved in your context?
- Is there furnishing in the chancel/sanctuary which is never used?
- How good are the sound system and the lighting?

Prayers of the people
- From where are the prayers of the people conducted?
- Does the position where the prayers are conducted help to underline the fact there these are the 'prayers of the people'?

Celebrating at the Lord's table
- How central is the Lord's Table to the worship assembly?
- Is there a visual balance between Lord's Table and the furniture used for the Word?
- Can a more central impact be created for the Lord's Table without significant re-ordering of the sanctuary, communion rails etc?
- If significant changes are necessary what implications are there for the rest of the sanctuary and chancel furnishings and even the body of the nave?

The place of baptism

- Is the font and surrounding area best suited for contemporary public baptismal liturgy?
- Does the position of the font denote entry into the Christian way?
- Could the font be a focus for the penitential section of the liturgy on occasion?
- Is there sufficient room for the assembly to gather around the font?
- Can a visual link be discerned between the positioning of the font, the lectern/pulpit and the holy table?
- Is care taken to avoid obscuring the purpose of the font by its manner of placing and decoration?

When seeking to answer any of the above questions there is a need to strike a balance between what might ideally suit the needs of Church of Ireland worship, in the context of the *BCP*, 2004, and the respect that it is necessary to have for the inherited shape and contents of the liturgical space, in the context of the local traditions of the worshipping congregation. It is recognized of course that churches differ in their layout and furnishings and that 'one size' does not necessarily 'fit all'. There may be a need to adapt the liturgy to the building as well as re-ordering the building for requirements of the liturgy. There will always be, in any case, an element of the ideal — what one would like to see to enable the liturgy to be presented in the best possible manner, and the practical — it may not even be physically possible to do everything that will facilitate 'best practice' with regard to the manner in which the church is ordered internally.

3
Practical Application

THE PRINCIPAL FOCAL POINTS in any Anglican Church will comprise the arrangements for Christian Initiation, specifically the placing and use of the font, the facilitation of the ministry of the Word and that of the Sacrament involving the lectern, pulpit and reading-desk, and the Holy Table. While items of furniture are themselves important, it is worth stating that their primary purpose is to draw appropriate attention to the items they carry or contain — notably Scripture, bread, wine and water.

The font
This should normally be situated at a single designated and visible place of baptism. Whether within the Church itself (as is the normal practice in the Church of Ireland) or in a separate annex to the main building, this place should have sufficient space to allow as many as possible of the congregation to gather with the candidates for baptism and their sponsors around the font, and to facilitate an orderly administration of the sacrament. Some sort of

visual connection between the two Gospel sacraments — baptism and Holy Communion — is helpful, the traditional arrangement being that the font is at or near the entrance to the church symbolizing admission to the Christian life, and the altar/table as representing the goal to which we aspire. Although some churches feature the font in the vicinity of the altar/table, this course of action should be undertaken cautiously as a visual confusion rather than a true relationship tends to occur.

The font, be it stone basin, pool or fountain, should normally be a permanent structure and may embody fundamental pieces of Christian symbolism. These could range from ancient carvings of fish or Noah's ark, for example, to the modern inclination to make the font coffin-like in shape so as to emphasize how in the deep waters of our baptism we must somehow share Christ's death in order to partake of his resurrection. It should facilitate the use of appropriately abundant quantities of water.

Focus of the Word
The proclaiming and receiving of the Word currently tends to be divided between three

visual centres, as follows:-

1. **The lectern**, from which the scriptures are read;
2. **The pulpit**, from which the sermon is preached;
3. **The reading desk** (a distinctive feature of Anglican worship), which is more suited to the 'Office' of Morning or Evening Prayer (Mattins and Evensong) than to the celebration of the Eucharist.

The conducting the first part of the Eucharist from the reading desk, and the second part at the Holy Table, can detract from the unity of Word and Sacrament. Some thought could be given to a revival of the ancient ambo (the single, slightly elevated place of the Word, which in the ancient Church was used for both reading and preaching) to serve as a single location from which the Scriptures may be read and preached and the ministry of the Word conducted. Given however the custom in some places of a Gospel procession to where the people are in the nave, it might be observed that this does not require any particular arrangement of furniture.

The place from which the Word is read and proclaimed, and where the Holy Bible is normally placed, should be a significant and permanent piece of liturgical furniture, and should not if at all practicable be used for other purposes. Both Word and sacrament have equal authority within Anglicanism and should have, so far as this can be ensured, equal status within Church of Ireland churches, as visually represented.

Leading prayer

The prayers of the people may be offered, depending on the layout of the church and constraints of audibility, from the aisle or in the midst of the people (the reading desk being traditionally used simply for the actual office of Morning and Evening Prayer). It is of course appropriate for people to lead the intercessions from their places in the nave. Above all, the intention must be to make clear that these are the prayers OF rather than FOR the people.

The Holy Table

This should be free-standing to enable the presiding bishop or priest to stand behind it, and where practical to allow the whole community to gather with him or her around it. This implies bringing the table out from the wall, and, in some instances, either into the middle of the chancel, or even into the nave. There should not, however, be more than one main altar/table in the body of the church

The presiding minister's chair
Ideally there should be a chair from which the liturgy is conducted visible to all and facing west behind the Holy Table. Although this is an important piece of liturgical furniture it should not be throne-like or over-stated, but should be of a kind to indicate the significance of the office of the liturgical president.

De-cluttering . . .
Churches should be uncluttered and a critical eye needs to be cast regularly and consideration given to removing furnishings and ornaments which have ceased to have any obvious purpose. Furthermore, an important part of any re-ordering must be for congregations to ask whether they need every conceivable space to be filled with pews. In larger churches, the possibility of having 'free' space in which people may assemble and also associate after acts

of worship, as well as having enough room to conduct processions, dramatized readings of the Scriptures, and the like, is of obvious value.

An apparently 'empty' space can itself be a symbol of the infinite majesty of God, and facilitate a feeling of peace and serenity in the midst of a busy and cluttered world. It follows that the manner of the ordering of a church also encourages moments of daily personal devotion, serving to remind us that liturgical space is not only crafted to address Sunday needs.

4
Wider Considerations

It would be prudent to acknowledge that parishes often give consideration to the re-ordering or adapting of liturgical space primarily in the context of other major work on the fabric of the building concerned. Often the desire to provide a kitchen and toilets, or an activity area for children, leads to a reduction in the area available for worship and a consequent interest in re-shaping it. While other considerations may serve as the catalyst leading to re-ordering for worship, the quality of the work subsequently carried out on the space retained for worship should not be ill-considered or compromised. While there have sometimes been cases where quite adventurous changes have been executed in relation to the multi-purpose use of buildings, the worship space has nevertheless been left rather drearily unaltered in a building which in other respects has had its essential proportions transformed.

If liturgical re-ordering is part of an overall scheme to adapt the interior of a church building, it should be noted that certain principles of good practice apply both to the liturgical work and to the more general scheme as well. The good practice principles to be applied are as follows:-

- In the case of heritage buildings, the work should, in theory, be reversible — at least to a degree that needs to be defined in consultation with the appropriate heritage authorities;
- A historic building will always include layers of evidence of the involvement of the local community with that building and when changes are being made this should be done in such a way as to avoid the permanent destruction of the legacy and work of a previous generation. In this context, the appropriate storage of valuable items no longer required *in situ* will need to be considered;
- Those contemplating re-ordering need to identify the special features of design and furnishing that are site-specific to that particular place, so that, over and above more general considerations, a special effort is made to cherish and conserve these unique features;

- Most worthwhile contemporary contributions to an older building will be made in the authentic idiom of today rather than in a manner that imitates the styles of the past;
- It is therefore important that consideration be given also to the incorporation of evidence of artistic excellence from our own time as well as from previous generations;
- Into both the fabric and the contents of the building careful consideration needs to be given to the conservation of existing fixed items, e.g. stained glass and significant monuments, which find themselves within a multi-purpose area;
- In any project, the brief given to the architect should include clear liturgical objectives so that they may be assisted in gauging the appropriate level of intervention to achieve such objectives. It is acknowledged that in buildings deemed to be of national importance such intervention will need to be minimal, but it is actually still possible to be liturgically radical whilst making minimal permanent impact on the fabric;
- There is a moral imperative on the Church to ensure that all adaptations to buildings, particularly in relation to matters such as

heating and choice of materials, be executed in the most environmentally-sensitive manner.

One often hears it said that adaptations to church buildings, whether for liturgical or other practical reasons, cannot easily be made because the planners or the conservation authorities will not permit such change. In many cases this is more an excuse to justify timid conservatism amongst parishioners than an accurate reflection of the views of the statutory authorities themselves. Our consultations with those authorities have made us aware that it remains quite possible to make radical alterations to heritage and protected structures, provided that these alterations are carried out with sensitivity and wisdom and according to due process in the appropriate jurisdiction.

Heritage authorities will be aware that churches are living places which of necessity change through the years, and that if those who use them and maintain them for their original and essential purpose are not permitted to alter them reasonably to meet the needs of the times, they may simply walk away from them and build new multi-purpose buildings from scratch. Such a scenario might then result in the original church passing into new ownership and being in the possession of persons who would make far more radical and insensitive requests to planning authorities than the previous ecclesiastical owners.

The other factor, over and above congenital caution, which makes congregations disinclined to contemplate radical work on church buildings, is a not ill-founded view concerning high costs. High-quality materials have to be used, while the requirements of current fire regulations in such contexts are very demanding indeed.

Having admitted this, however, the over-riding argument and indeed duty to enrich what are often old structures to meet the needs of the people of God in our time, are very strong indeed. Sites with a long continuity of worship and witness have obvious significance in our communities today. Our predecessors of past centuries, usually with the best of motives, spent vast sums on the construction and adornment of our notable buildings. Those who will follow us will deserve to find evidence that ours too was an era of generosity, creativity and excellence, as well as one of maintenance – an era in which the self-understanding of God's people was clearly articulated through their worship, and in which the dialogue between beauty and holiness remained constant.

Bibliography & Resources

THE RCB LIBRARY IN DUBLIN is the official place of deposit for Church of Ireland records, and should be the first resort for information about access to such primary source records as architectural drawings, visitations and descriptive survey material, as well as printed parish histories and many of the resource books listed below.

For further information see the Library's webpages on the Church of Ireland website <http://www.library.ireland.anglican.org/>. Both the Irish Architectural Archive <www.iarc.ie> and the Public Record Office of Northern Ireland <www.proni.gov.uk> may also be useful.

An introduction to the types of records that can help reconstruct how churches were originally laid out was provided by Dr Susan Hood, in a presentation entitled 'Telling the "inside" story: archival sources for Church of Ireland interiors', delivered at the Department of Environment, Heritage and Local Government

(DEHLG) Seminar: *Inside the Place of Worship, Dublin Castle, 6 October 2009.* Visual and other historical resources from the presentation are available at this link:
<http://www.ireland.anglican.org/index.php?do=about&id=94>

The following printed works are also available in the RCB Library:

Select materials relating to the historical layout of church buildings

G.W.O. Addleshaw and Frederick Etchells, *The Architectural Setting of Anglican Worship* (Faber and Faber, London, 1948)

Maurice Craig, *The Architecture of Ireland From the Earliest Times to 1880* (Eason, Dublin,1982)

John Crawford, *The Church of Ireland in Victorian Dublin*, especially chapter 4: 'The church, church services and religious practice', pp. 122-150 (Four Courts Press, Dublin, 2005)

Sam Hutchinson, *Towers, Spires and Pinnacles: A History of the Cathedrals and Churches of the Church of Ireland* (Wordwell, Bray, 2003)

Paul Larmour and Stephen McBride, 'Buildings and faith: church building from medieval to modern', in Raymond Gillespie and W. G. Neely (eds.), *The Laity and the Church of Ireland 1000-2000* (Four Courts Press, Dublin, 2002), pp. 304-350

David Lee and Debbie Jacobs, *James Pain Architect* (Limerick Civic Trust, Limerick, 2005)

Edward Norman, *The House of God: Church Architecture, Style and History* (Thames and Hudson, London, 1990)

Richard Oram, *Expressions of Faith: Ulster's Church Heritage* (Colourprint, Newtownards, 2001)

Simon Walker, *Historic Ulster Churches* (UAHS, Belfast, 2000)

H.A. Wheeler and M.J. Craig, *The Dublin City Churches of the Church of Ireland* (APCK, Dublin, 1948)

Nigel Yates, *Liturgical Space: Christian Worship and Church Buildings in Western Europe 1500-2000, Liturgy, Worship and Society* (Ashgate, Aldershot, 2008)

Nigel Yates, *Buildings, Faith and Worship: The*

Liturgical Arrangement of Anglican Churches 1600-1900, revised edition (Oxford University Press, Oxford, 2000)

Select materials relating to liturgical space

Note: texts marked * deal particularly with the practical and theological questions of (re)-ordering space

Peter Frederick Anson, *Fashions in Church Furnishings, 1840-1940*, second edition, (Studio Vista, London, 1965)

P.H. Ballard, (ed.), *The Church at the Centre of the City* (Epworth, London, 2008)

Frank Bottomley, *The Church Explorer's Guide to Symbols and their Meaning* (Kaye and Ward, London, 1978)

Gilbert Cope, *Making the Building Serve the Liturgy: Studies in the Re-ordering of Churches* (Mobray and Co., London, 1962)

Patricia Dirsztay, *Inside Churches: A Guide to Church Furnishings* (National Association of Decorative & Fine Arts Societies, London, 1993)

*R. Gibbons, *House of God: House of the People of God: A Study of Christian Liturgical Space*, Alcuin Club Collections 82 (SPCK, London, 2006)

R. Giles, *Creating Uncommon Worship: Transforming the Liturgy of the Eucharist* (Canterbury, Norwich, 2004)

*R. Giles, *Re-pitching the Tent: The Definitive Guide to Re-ordering Church Buildings for Worship and Mission*, third edition (Canterbury, Norwich, 2004)

J. A. Inge, *Christian Theology of Place: Explorations in Practical, Pastoral and Empirical Theology* (Ashgate, Aldershot, 2003)

*P. North, and J. North, (eds.), *Sacred Space: House of God, Gate of Heaven* (Continuum, London, 2007)

Appendices

I Six practical steps for re-ordering of churches in the Republic of Ireland

The following are practical steps that parishes in the Republic of Ireland should undertake in order to comply with Church and State regulations when church building development or re-ordering is being contemplated:-

1. Appoint an architect with expertise in the conservation of historic buildings.

2. Establish if the church building is listed as a protected structure under the Planning and Development Acts.

3. Where any alteration in the structure, ornaments, furnishings or monuments of a church (whether by introduction, alteration or removal) is being contemplated, a Form of Consent to Alterations (available from the Representative Church Body) should be completed and the approval of the bishop or ordinary obtained.

4. Obtain the approval of the Diocesan Council and the Representative Church Body for

any works involved in the church building development that are not covered by the Form of Consent to Alterations.

5. Obtain the consent of the relevant Planning Authority to the proposed works, if applicable.

6. Refer to the Architectural Heritage Protection – *Guidelines for Planning Authorities: Places of Public Worship* chapter 5. Available on the Department of the Environment Heritage and Local Government website at:
 <www.environ.ie>.

II Seven practical steps for re-ordering of churches in Northern Ireland

The following are practical steps that parishes in Northern Ireland should undertake in order to comply with Church and State regulations when church building development or re-ordering is being contemplated:-

1. Appoint an architect with expertise in the conservation of historic buildings.

2. Establish if the church building is a listed building.

3. Where any alteration in the structure, ornaments, furnishings or monuments of a church (whether by introduction, alteration or removal) is being contemplated, a Form of Consent to Alterations (available from the Representative Church Body) should be completed and the approval of the bishop or ordinary obtained.

4. Obtain the approval of the Diocesan Council and the Representative Church Body for any works involved in the church building

development that are not covered by the Form of Consent to Alterations.

5. Alterations to churches are subject to the same planning requirements for obtaining planning permission as unlisted buildings but 'the ecclesiastical exemption' applies to the interior and therefore a listed building consent is not required. It is recommended, however, that NIEA Built Heritage should be consulted before (any) alterations are made.

6. Obtain the consent of the relevant Planning Authority to the proposed works, if applicable.

7. Refer to the Department of the Environment Built Heritage website at: <www.ehsni.gov.uk>.